World Wonders

"Hiya, I'm Zeek."

"Hi, I'm Finn."

Calling all aliens!

Are you planning a holiday to planet Earth?

Finn and Zeek are here to help.

'World Wonders'
Published by MAVERICK ARTS PUBLISHING LTD

Studio 11, City Business Centre, 6 Brighton Road,
Horsham, West Sussex, RH13 5BB, +44 (0)1403 256941
© Maverick Arts Publishing Limited November 2019

A CIP catalogue record for this book is available at the British Library.

ISBN 978-1-84886-635-5

Maverick publishing
www.maverickbooks.co.uk

Credits:

Finn & Zeek illustrations by Jake McDonald, Bright Illustration Agency
Cover: Jake McDonald/Bright, Miles Ertman/Robertharding.com.
Inside: **Robertharding.com:** Andrew Michael (6), Gavin Hellier (8), Kerstin Langenberger (9), Nigel Hicks (10), Bill Ward (10), Christian Handl (12), NPS Photo Archive (13), Marco Brivio (13, 15), Matthias Graben (16), Jose Fuste Raga (17), ES Imagery (17), Helmut Corneli (19), Robert Francis (20), Robert Harding Productions (21), Ashley Cooper (21), Alexander Van Driessche (22), Matthew Williams-Ellis (23, 28), Miles Ertman (24), David Jacobs (27), Tony Waltham (27). **Shutterstock:** Rafael Ben-Ari (18), Tanya Puntti (18), Gallinago_media (23).

Gold

This book is rated as: Gold Band (Guided Reading)

World Wonders

Contents

Introduction	6
Remarkable Rocks	8
Fairy Chimneys	8
The Giant's Causeway	10
Wonderful Water	12
Hot Springs	12
Geysers	14
Waterfalls	16
Unique Underwater	18
Coral	18
Tough Trees	20
Strangler Figs	20
Underground	22
The Crystal Cave	22
Waitomo Glowworm Caves	23
Stunning Skies	24
Aurora	24
Quiz	28
Index/Glossary	30

Hello fellow aliens! What do you want to know about planet Earth?

INCOMING MESSAGE

Dear Finn and Zeek

We're off on a trip to Earth soon, and we want to see something a bit weird and unusual. Which places on Earth will 'wow' us?

Yours,
Kewl, Asa, Cumber
(Planet Oooo)

Introduction

The Earth has some amazing natural sights. Some can be explained. Others are still a bit of a mystery!

G'day mate! We're here in Australia.

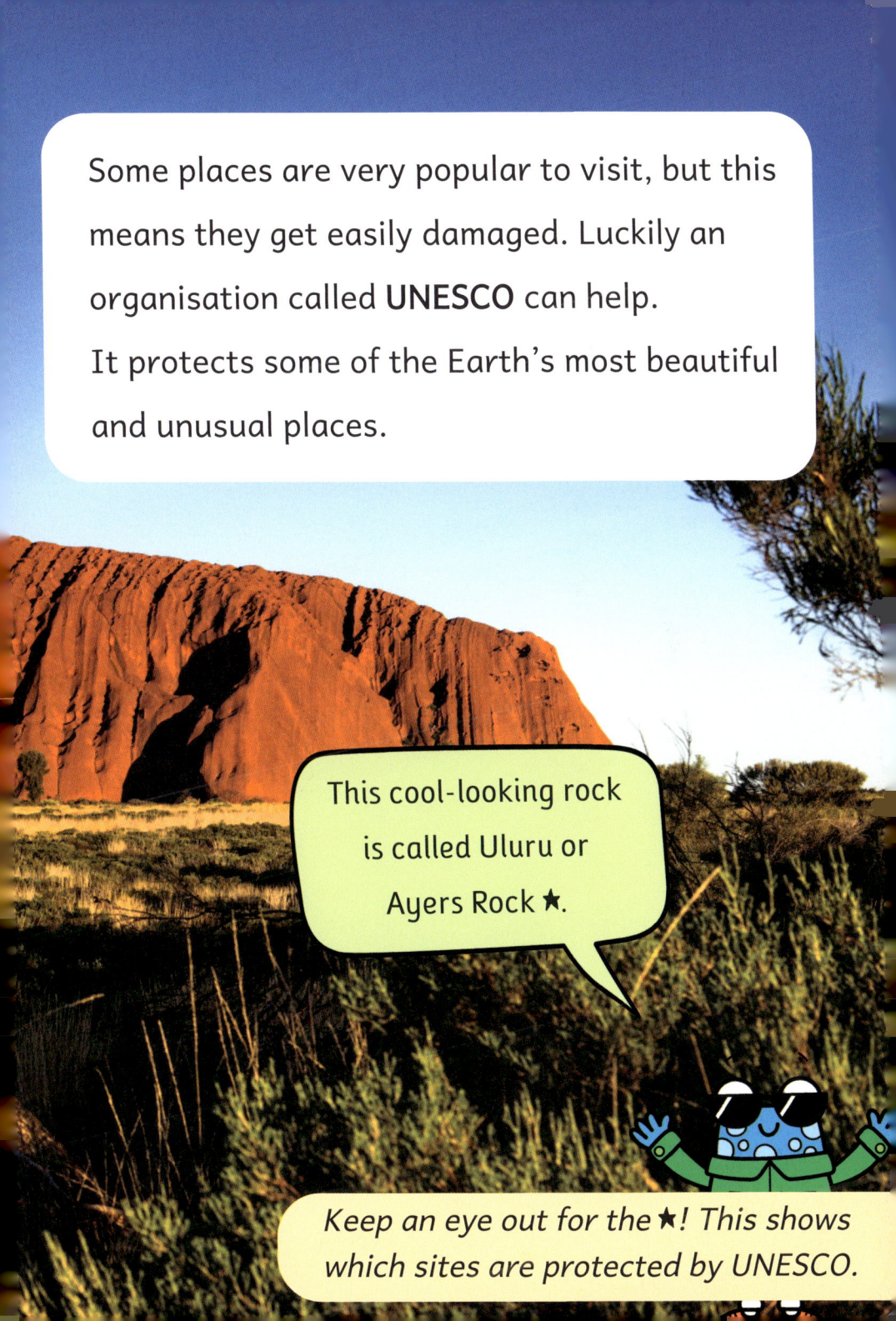

Some places are very popular to visit, but this means they get easily damaged. Luckily an organisation called **UNESCO** can help.
It protects some of the Earth's most beautiful and unusual places.

This cool-looking rock is called Uluru or Ayers Rock ★.

Keep an eye out for the ★! This shows which sites are protected by UNESCO.

Remarkable Rocks | Fairy Chimneys ★

Rocks are all round, grey and boring... wrong! There are some remarkable rocks on Earth.

These rocks in Cappadocia, Turkey, look like chimneys. They look magical, but there is a scientific reason for how they look.

Basalt

Tuff

Thousands of years ago, volcanoes erupted. The ash from the volcanoes became soft rock called '**tuff**'. This was then covered by a layer of harder rock called '**basalt**'. Wind and rain wear away tuff quicker than basalt, leaving the mushroom shape at the top!

Ash

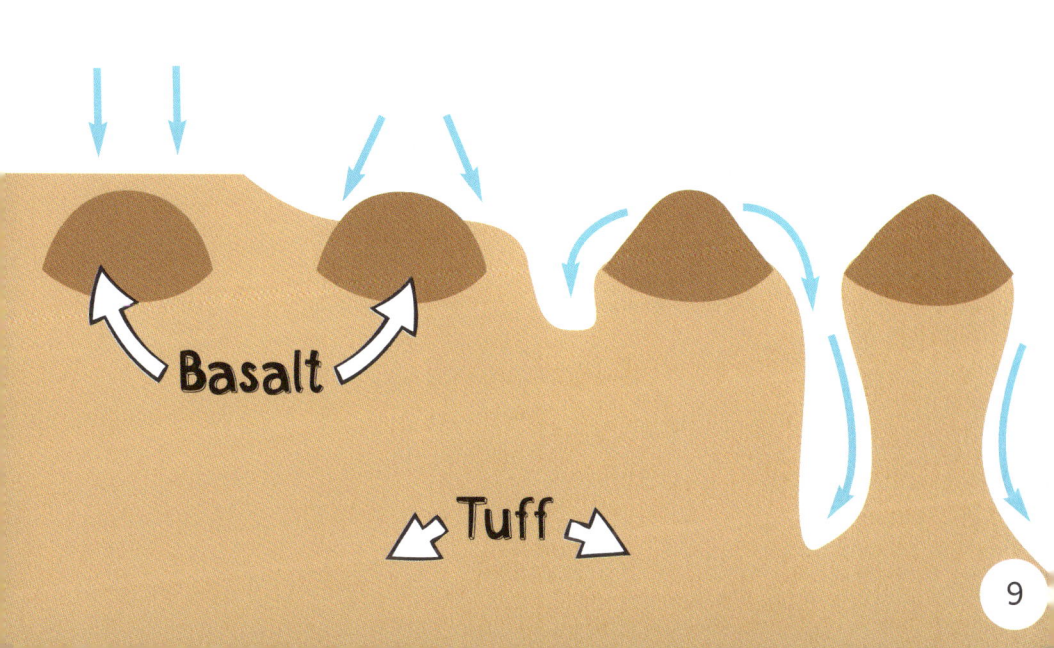

Basalt

Tuff

Remarkable Rocks The Giant's Causeway ★

There is a story that says this **causeway** of rocks was created by a giant!

However, like the fairy chimneys, it was really caused by volcanic eruptions millions of years ago. The lava erupted onto the Earth's surface. As it cooled, basalt was formed. This basalt contracted, creating the unusual shapes.

The rocks are hexagonal in shape.

Wonderful Water — Hot Springs

Yellowstone Park ★ in the USA is famous for its hot springs. The hot springs are made when water from the surface goes deep down undergound. When it reaches hot **magma**, the water heats up and makes its way back to the surface. This makes a pool.

The bright colours in a hot spring are due to the **bacteria** living in the water.

Although the blue water looks lovely, it is dangerous to swim in it!

Grand Prismatic Spring

1966

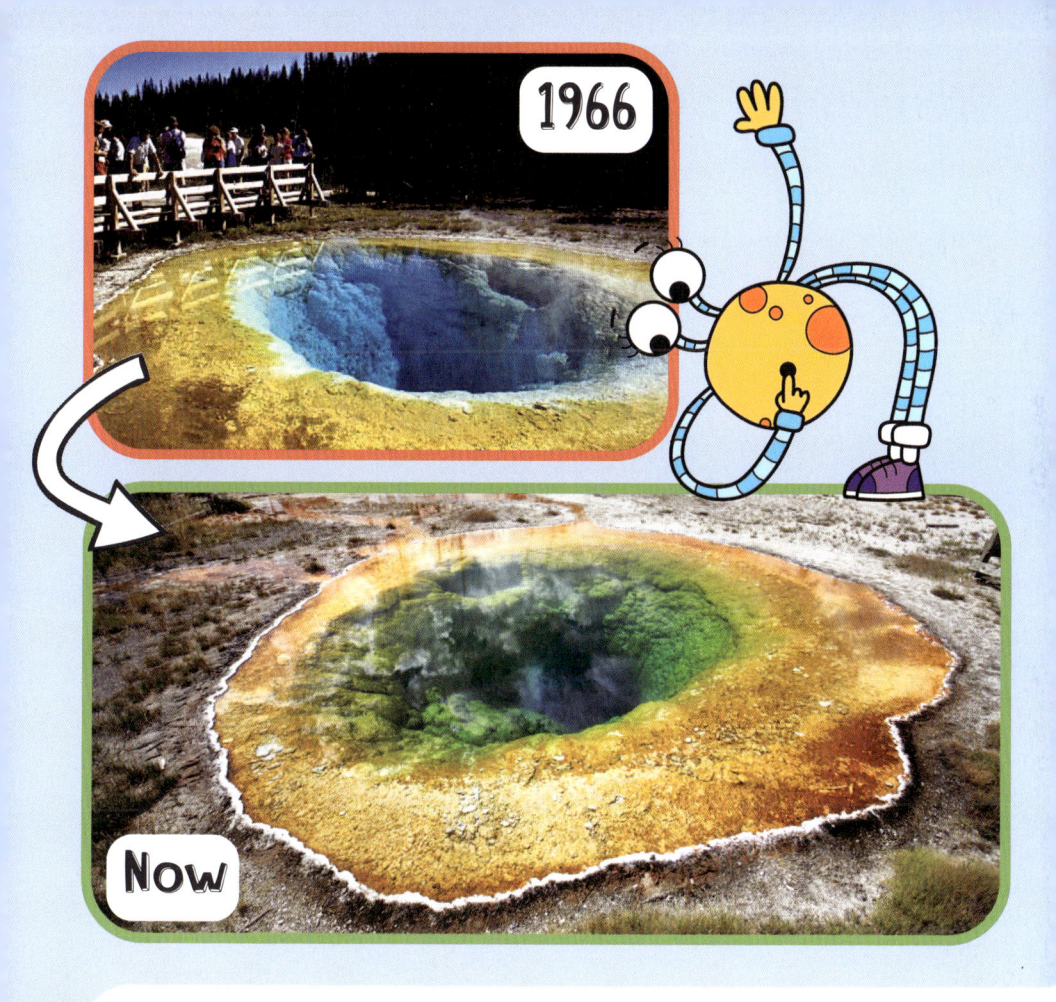

Now

Morning Glory Pool

This hot spring used to be bright blue. However, people used to throw rubbish into the spring. This upset the balance of bacteria, and changed the pool's colour.

Wonderful Water   Geysers

Hold onto your hats! When water gets trapped underground, it turns into steam. The **pressure** builds up and the steam is forced to the surface. Big bursts of steam like this are called geysers.

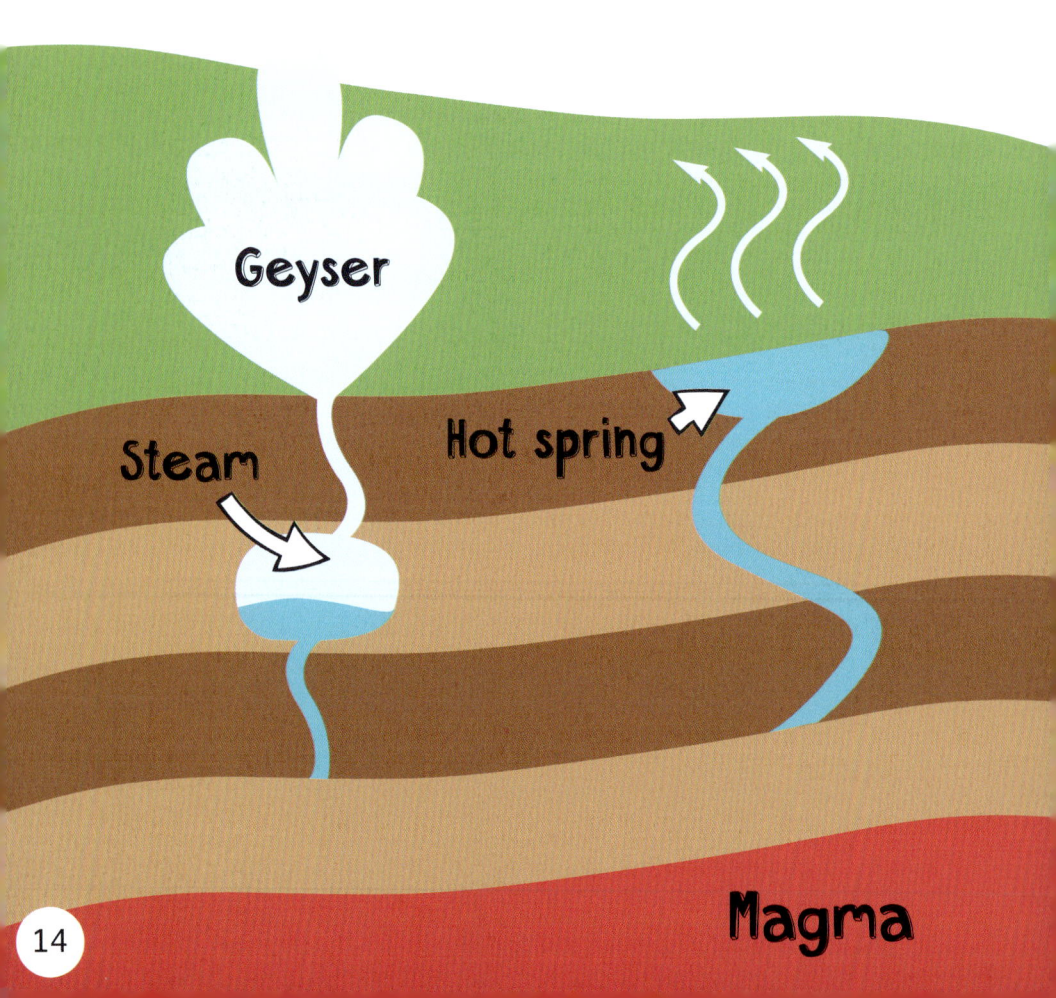

Geyser

Steam

Hot spring

Magma

This is the Old Faithful geyser, at Yellowstone Park. It is well-named: it erupts faithfully every hour!

Wonderful Water — Waterfalls

Iguazu Falls (South America) ★

Earth's biggest waterfalls provide a treat for the senses! Victoria Falls is in Africa, Niagara Falls is between Canada and the USA, and Iguazu Falls is in South America. They are big, loud and very wet!

Niagra Falls, USA & Canada ★

Victoria Falls, Africa ★

1. Hard rock
2. Soft rock
3. Ledge

Waterfalls are made when water flows over rock. The softer rock wears away more quickly and the hard rock is left hanging. This leaves a ledge for the water to 'fall' off.

Unique Underwater Coral

The Great Barrier Reef

The Great Barrier Reef ★ in Australia looks like it is made up of rock, but it's actually alive!

It is made of coral, which is a living thing that has a hard, stony surface. All kinds of underwater creatures live in coral reefs.

18

The temperature of the sea is rising because of **climate change**. This means that coral is in danger. When it gets too warm, the coral '**bleaches**' and can die. One day, coral may be extinct!

That doesn't look good.

Tough Trees   Strangler Figs

Humans are always cutting down trees to use the wood, but in some places the trees are fighting back! In Krong Siem Reap, Cambodia, the strangler fig trees have taken over the ancient temple buildings.

Strangler fig seeds are left behind by animals. If a seed is left in another tree, then the strangler fig's roots grow around the older tree. When the older tree dies, it leaves a hollow centre. It certainly makes for a weird sight!

(★ The man-made temples are protected by UNESCO but not the trees!)

Underground

The Crystal Cave, Naica Mine

Human for scale

The Crystal Cave in Mexico is home to the biggest crystals ever discovered. The largest are around 11 metres long! The Crystal Cave was discovered in 2000 when miners pumped out water. However in 2017, the cave was filled with water again to keep the crystals safe.

Waitomo Glowworm Caves

In the Waitomo Caves, New Zealand, it looks like the night sky if you look up. However, the things that look like stars are really glowworms! They like the dark, and they get food from the river that runs through the caves.

Glowworms are actually **larvae** of fungus gnats. They create webs like spiders. They create a glow to attract prey to their webs.

Glowworm

Stunning Skies   Aurora

The Aurora happens when particles from the sun hit each other as they enter the earth's atmosphere.

If you want to see something truly magical, go to the Arctic or Antarctic. There, you might see the Auroras. These are natural light displays in the sky.

MESSAGE SENT

Dear Kewl, Asa and Cumber,

Earth has some amazing natural places to see. There really are too many to tell you about! We've included photos of some others that you could look up.

Remember, if you visit any of these sites, don't leave any litter or take anything away. We want aliens and humans of the future to enjoy these wondrous sites!

From,
Finn and Zeek x

Wave Rock, Australia

Stone Forest, China

Quiz

1. Which human organisation protects natural sites of interest?
a) UNESCO
b) WWP
c) The Site Protection Society

2. What is the soft rock in the fairy chimneys called?
a) Maff
b) Tuff
c) Dall

3. What causes these glowing webs?

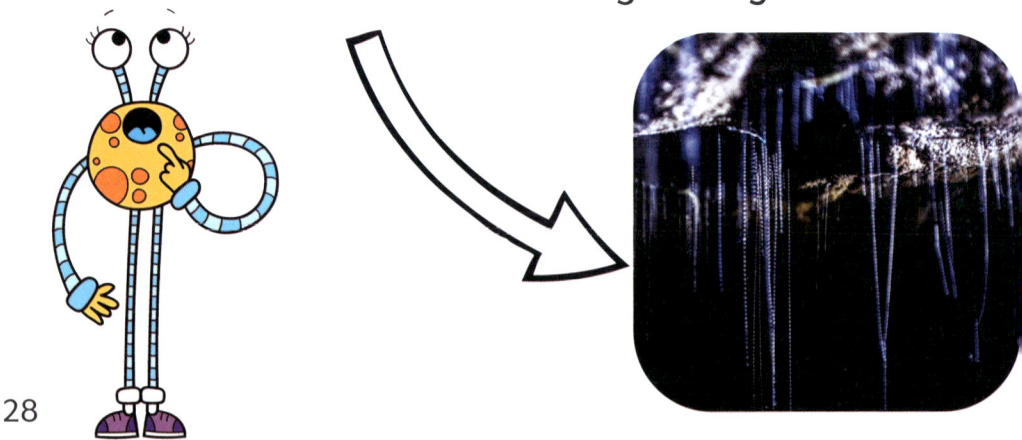

4. What causes the bleaching of coral?
a) The sea cooling down
b) The sea warming up
c) Humans breaking the coral

5. Which one of these is not a waterfall?
a) Niagra
b) Victoria
c) Horatio

6. Where is the Old Faithful geyser found?
a) Blue Lagoon
b) Redrock Reserve
c) Yellowstone Park

Turn over for answers

Index/Glossary

Bacteria pg 12, 13

Bacteria are tiny life forms made of one cell. They can't be seen without a microscope, but they are everywhere!

Basalt pg 8, 9, 11

A hard volcanic rock. It is dark in colour.

Bleaches/Bleaching pg 19

When the sea water becomes too warm, the coral turns white. The coral can recover from this if the environment changes for the better.

Causeway pg 10

A raised road across wet ground.

Climate change pg 19

A change in the Earth's temperature caused, at least partly, by things that humans do.

Quiz Answers:
1. a, 2. b, 3. Glowworms (or larvae of gnats),
4. b, 5. c, 6. c

Larva/ Larvae pg 23

These are the young forms of insects. They are wingless and can look a bit like worms.

Magma pg 12, 14

A very hot liquid found within the Earth's crust.

Pressure pg 14

The force with which a liquid or gas pushes against something.

Tuff pg 8, 9

A soft rock made from volcanic ash.

UNESCO pg 7, 21

This stands for 'The United Nations Educational, Scientific and Cultural Organisation'. This organisation decides which sites will become World Heritage Sites. These are protected sites which are important, special or beautiful.

31

Book Bands for Guided Reading

The Institute of Education book banding system is a scale of colours that reflects the various levels of reading difficulty. The bands are assigned by taking into account the content, the language style, the layout and phonics. Word, phrase and sentence level work is also taken into consideration.

Maverick Early Readers are a bright, attractive range of books covering the pink to white bands. All of these books have been book banded for guided reading to the industry standard and edited by a leading educational consultant.

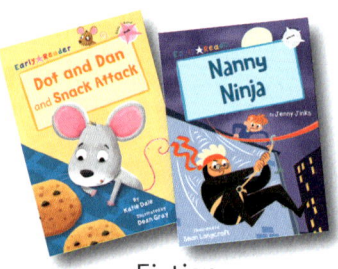

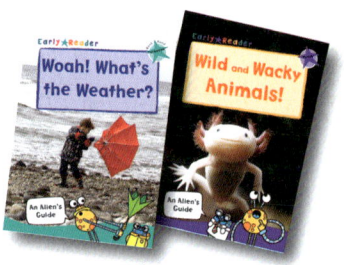

Fiction

Non-fiction

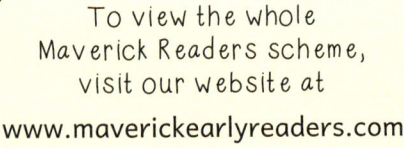

To view the whole Maverick Readers scheme, visit our website at www.maverickearlyreaders.com

Or scan the QR code above to view our scheme instantly!